The Christn Carol Book

29 Popular Carols with words & music

Chosen and arranged
by Brian V. Burdett MA (OXON)
in collaboration with
Shirley M. Sturgeon LRAM ARCM

Introduction

In this book we have brought together twenty-nine of the best known and most popular Christmas Carols with their traditional tunes which have stood the test of time. We have added straightforward arrangements which the average 'family' pianist will be able to manage without difficulty.

The early traditions of the carol are closely associated with the dance and it is this very vitality and rhythm which distinguishes them from hymns. We have tried to retain this cheerful spirit by the use of colour illustrations throughout the book.

The 'pocket' size was chosen for the convenience of carollers who may want to carry the book from place to place. The words have been set out with the real needs of the singer in mind.

The book is primarily intended for use by families at home or larger groups of non-professionals, either in or out of doors. However, the content and standard are such that it should also be useful to more serious musicians.

A MERRY CHRISTMAS

Words Anonymous

Traditional West Country
Arranged by B. V. Burdett

Permision to publish this simplified version of Arthur Warrell's arrangement given by Oxford University Press

A MERRY CHRISTMAS

1. We wish you a merry Christmas,
   We wish you a merry Christmas,
   We wish you a merry Christmas,
   And a happy New Year.

   Chorus:
   Good tidings we bring
   To you and your kin,
   We wish you a merry Christmas,
   And a happy New Year.

2. Now bring us some figgy pudding,
   Now bring us some figgy pudding,
   Now bring us some figgy pudding,
   And bring some out here.

   Chorus:

3. For we all like figgy pudding,
   For we all like figgy pudding,
   For we all like figgy pudding,
   So bring some out here.

   Chorus:

4. And we won't go until we've got
   some,
   And we won't go until we've got
   some,
   And we won't go until we've got
   some,
   So bring some out here.

   Chorus:

ANGELS, FROM THE REALMS OF GLORY

Words by James Montgomery
1771–1854

Traditional French tune

*This tune is an old French carol 'Les Anges dans nos campagnes'.
James Montgomery's words appear to be an early nineteenth-century
translation of the French carol and first appeared in print in 1816 and
later in 1825 in a book called* The Christmas Box. *The words of the
fifth verse come from a different carol in that same publication.*

From the *Oxford Book of Carols* by permission of Oxford University Press

Coventry Cathedral

Angels, from the Realms of Glory

Angels, from the realms of glory,
  Wing your flight o'er all the earth;
Ye who sang creation's story
  Now proclaim Messiah's birth:
    Gloria in excelsis Deo.

Shepherds in the field abiding,
  Watching o'er your flocks by night,
God with man is now residing;
  Yonder shines the infant light:
    Gloria in excelsis Deo.

Sages, leave your contemplations;
  Brighter visions beam afar;
Seek the great desire of nations;
  Ye have seen his natal star:
    Gloria in excelsis Deo.

Saints before the altar bending,
  Watching long in hope and fear,
Suddenly the Lord, descending,
  In his temple shall appear:
    Gloria in excelsis Deo.

Though an infant now we view him,
  He shall fill his Father's throne,
Gather all the nations to him;
  Every knee shall then bow down:
    Gloria in excelsis Deo.

Away in a Manger

Away in a manger, no crib for a bed,
The little Lord Jesus laid down his sweet head,
The stars in the bright sky looked down where he lay,
The little Lord Jesus asleep on the hay.

The cattle are lowing, the baby awakes,
But the little Lord Jesus, no crying he makes.
I love thee, Lord Jesus, look down from the sky,
And stay by my side until morning is nigh.

Be near me, Lord Jesus; I ask thee to stay
Close by me for ever, and love me, I pray.
Bless all the dear children in thy tender care.
And fit us for heaven to live with thee there.

AWAY IN A MANGER

Words Anonymous

Tune by William James Kirkpatrick 1838–1921
Arranged by B. V. Burdett

*The writer of these words is not known, but they are thought to
have been written for an American Sunday School class. This tune,
with which the words are most frequently associated, was also written
by an American, William James Kirkpatrick (1838–1921), a composer and director
of church music.*

*St Paul's Cathedral – traditional crib
as used in days gone by.*

DECK THE HALL
WITH BOUGHS OF HOLLY

Words Traditional

Traditional Welsh Tune
Arranged by B. V. Burdett

The words and the tune 'Hobaderry danno' are both Welsh traditional. It was collected by T. Oliphant (1799–1873), and with its reference to both Christmas and the New Year has become a firm favourite.

Westminster Abbey

Deck the Hall with Boughs of Holly

Deck the hall with boughs of holly,
Fa la la la la, fa la la la.
'Tis the season to be jolly,
Fa la la la la, fa la la la.
Fill the mead cup, drain the barrel,
Fa la la la la, fa la la la,
Troll the ancient Christmas carol,
Fa la la la la, fa la la la.

See the blazing Yule before us,
Fa la la la la, fa la la la.
Strike the harp and join the chorus,
Fa la la la la, fa la la la.
Follow me in merry measure,
Fa la la la la, fa la la la.
While I sing of Yuletide's treasure,
Fa la la la la, fa la la la.

Fast away the old year passes,
Fa la la la la, fa la la la.
Hail the new, ye lads and lasses,
Fa la la la la, fa la la la.
Sing we joyous, all together,
Fa la la la la, fa la la la.
Heedless of the wind and weather,
Fa la la la la, fa la la la.

Ding Dong!
Merrily on High

Ding dong! merrily on high
In heav'n the bells are ringing:
Ding dong! verily the sky
Is riv'n with angels singing.
> Gloria, Hosanna in excelsis!

E'en so here below, below,
Let steeple bells be swungen,
And i—o, i—o, i—o,
By priest and people sungen.
> Gloria, Hosanna in excelsis!

Pray you, dutifully prime
Your matin chime, ye ringers;
May you beautifully rime
Your eve-time song, ye singers.
> Gloria, Hosanna in excelsis!

DING DONG! MERRILY ON HIGH

Words by G. R. Woodward
1859–1934

Traditional French tune
Arranged by Charles Wood
Adapted by B. V. Burdett

The words are by G. R. Woodward (1859–1934) and are therefore not as old as they seem. The tune is a delightful sixteenth-century French dance tune (Branle) from Arbeau's Orchesographie *of 1588. This type of dance was quick and lively with two heavy beats for 'joined feet and a high jump'.*

By permission of the S.P.C.K.

Norwich Cathedral

GOD REST YOU MERRY

Words from William Sandys
Christmas Carols 1833

Traditional tune
Arranged by B. V. Burdett

*A very popular traditional English carol. There is a version
of it dating from about 1770. The words here are taken from William
Sandys's* Christmas Carols *(1833). The tune is taken from a broadsheet
printed in London about the beginning of the nineteenth century.*

God Rest You Merry

1. God rest you merry, gentlemen,
   Let nothing you dismay,
   For Jesus Christ our Saviour
   Was born upon this day,
   To save us all from Satan's power
   When we were gone astray:
       O tidings of comfort and joy.

2. From God our heavenly Father
   A blessèd angel came,
   And unto certain shepherds
   Brought tidings of the same,
   How that in Bethlehem was born
   The Son of God by name:
       O tidings of comfort and joy.

3. The shepherds at those tidings
   Rejoicèd much in mind,
   And left their flocks a-feeding,
   In tempest, storm and wind,
   And went to Bethlehem straightaway
   This blessèd babe to find:
       O tidings of comfort of joy.

4. But when to Bethlehem they came,
   Whereat this infant lay,
   They found him in a manger,
   Where oxen feed on hay;
   His mother Mary kneeling,
   Unto the Lord did pray:
       O tidings of comfort and joy.

5. Now to the Lord sing praises,
   All you within this place,
   And with true love and brotherhood
   Each other now embrace;
   This holy tide of Christmas
   All others doth deface:
       O tidings of comfort and joy.

GOOD KING WENCESLAS

Words by J. M. Neale
1818–1866

Tune from *Piae Cantiones*
Harmonised by Sir John Stainer
1840–1901

*This deservedly popular tune is a thirteenth-century spring dance carol.
Dr J. M. Neale put his own words to the tune (1853) which was popularised
by Bramley and Stainer (Christmas Carols, 1867). The moral tale and
the general sentiment of these words do not fit the rhythm and style of
the tune but it is unlikely that they can be separated now.*

Champéry, Switzerland
Swiss National Tourist Office

Good King Wenceslas

Good King Wenceslas looked out
  On the Feast of Stephen,
When the snow lay round about,
  Deep, and crisp, and even:
Brightly shone the moon that night,
  Though the frost was cruel,
When a poor man came in sight,
  Gathering winter fuel.

'Hither, page, and stand by me,
  If thou know'st it, telling,
Yonder peasant, who is he?
  Where and what his dwelling?'
'Sire, he lives a good league hence,
  Underneath the mountain,
Right against the forest fence,
  By Saint Agnes' fountain.'

'Bring me flesh, and bring me wine,
  Bring me pine-logs hither:
Thou and I will see him dine,
  When we bear them thither.'
Page and monarch, forth they went,
  Forth they went together;
Through the rude wind's wild lament
  And the bitter weather.

'Sire, the night is darker now,
  And the wind blows stronger;
Fails my heart, I know not how;
  I can go no longer.'
'Mark my footsteps, good my page;
  Tread thou in them boldly:
Thou shalt find the winter's rage
  Freeze thy blood less coldly.'

In his master's steps he trod,
  Where the snow lay dinted;
Heat was in the very sod
  Which the saint had printed.
Therefore, Christian men, be sure,
  Wealth or rank possessing,
Ye who now will bless the poor,
  Shall yourselves find blessing.

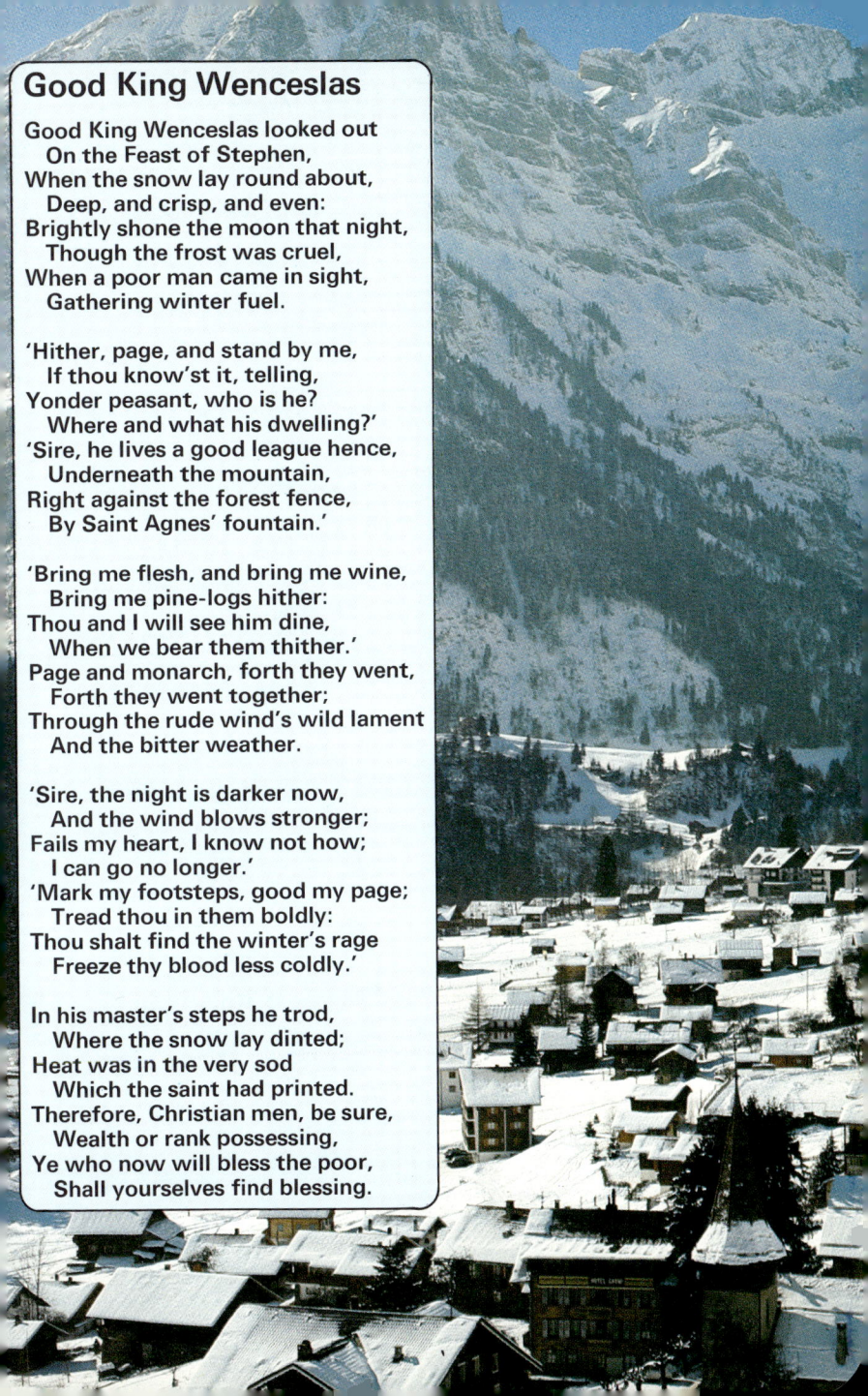

HARK! THE HERALD ANGELS SING

Words by C. Wesley 1707–1788. G. Whitefield 1714–1770
M. Madan 1726–1790 and others.

Tune by Mendelssohn
1809–1847

The words first appeared in Hymns and Sacred Poems *(1739). The tune
was adapted from a chorus by Mendelssohn and most suitably matches
Wesley's words, though Mendelssohn felt the tune 'unsuitable for sacred
words'. The verses as they now appear are in fact the work of several
writers.*

Sunset over Skye

Hark! The
Herald Angels Sing

Hark ! the herald angels sing
Glory to the new-born King;
Peace on earth and mercy mild,
God and sinners reconciled:
Joyful all ye nations rise,
Join the triumph of the skies,
With the angelic host proclaim,
Christ is born in Bethlehem
      Hark! the Herald angels sing
      Glory to the new-born King.

Christ, by highest heav'n adored,
Christ, the everlasting Lord,
Late in time behold him come
Offspring of a Virgin's womb:
Veiled in flesh the Godhead see,
Hail the incarnate Deity!
Pleased as man with man to dwell,
Jesus, our Emmanuel.
      Hark! the herald angels sing
      Glory to the new-born King.

Hail the heav'n-born Prince of Peace!
Hail the Sun of Righteousness!
Light and life to all he brings,
Risen with healing in his wings;
Mild he lays his glory by,
Born that man no more may die,
Born to raise the sons of earth,
Born to give them second birth.
      Hark! the herald angels sing
      Glory to the new-born King.

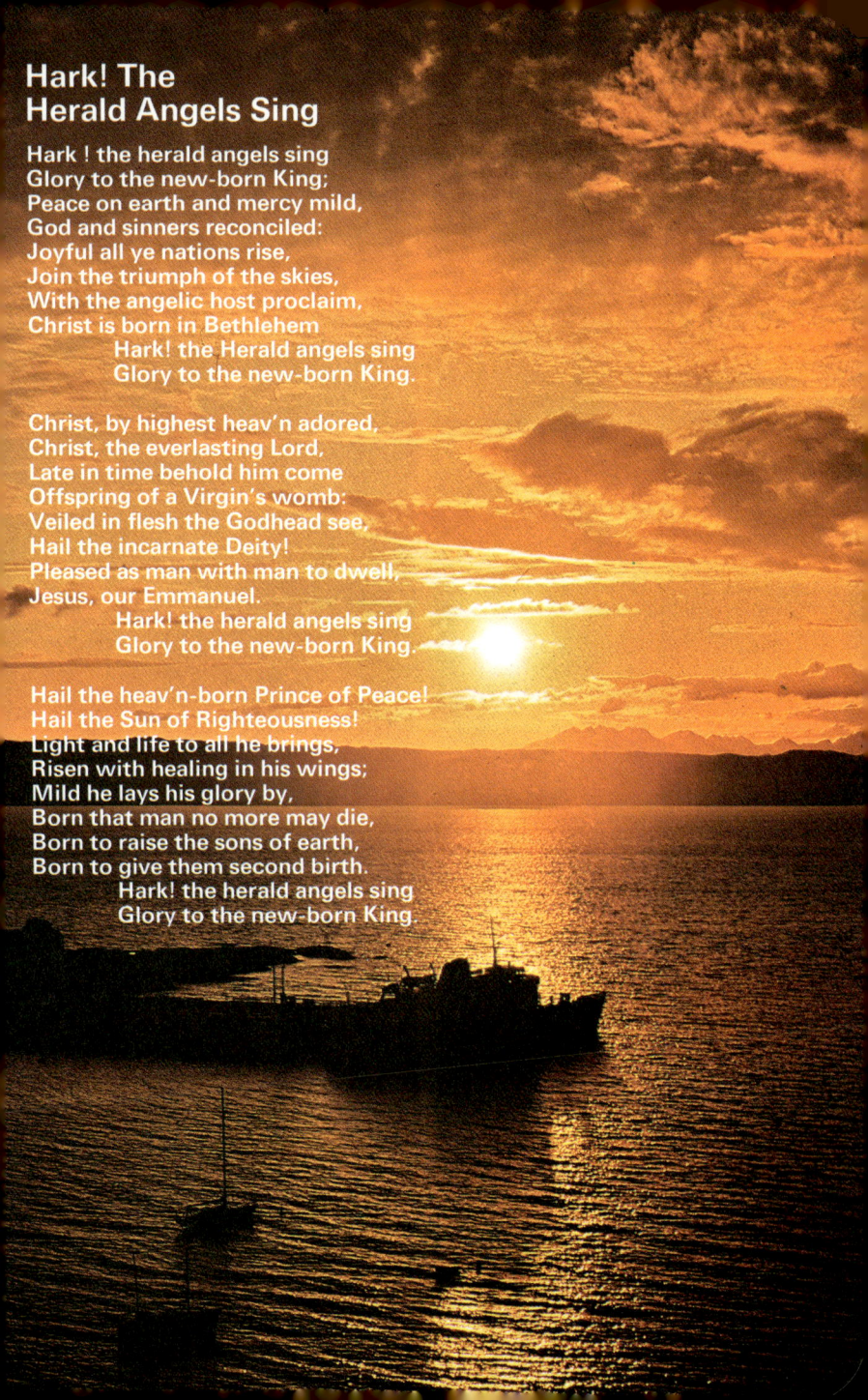

Here We Come a-Wassailing

Here we come a-wassailing
Among the leaves so green,
Here we come a-wandering,
So fair to be seen:

Chorus:
Love and joy come to you,
And to you your wassail too,
And God bless you, and send you
A happy new year,
And God send you
A happy new year.

We are not daily beggars
That beg from door to door,
But we are neighbours' children
Whom you have seen before:

Chorus:

We have got a little purse
Of stretching leather skin;
We want a little of your money
To line it well within:

Chorus:

Bring us out a table,
And spread it with a cloth;
Bring us out a mouldy cheese,
And some of your Christmas loaf:

Chorus:

God bless the master of this house,
Likewise the mistress too;
And all the little children
That round the table go:

Chorus:

Good Master and good Mistress,
While you're sitting by the fire,
Pray think of us poor children
Who are wandering in the mire:

Chorus:

HERE WE COME A-WASSAILING

Words from Husk, *Songs of the Nativity, 1868*

Traditional tune from Yorkshire
Arranged by B. V. Burdett

This tune from Yorkshire has become well known through its inclusion in
Christmas Carols New & Old, 1867. *The words come from* Songs of the
Nativity, 1868. *Reference is made there to a Yorkshire copy of the carol in a
broad sheet printed at Bradford as late as 1850. There is however, some
evidence to suggest that some of the verses may come from a source dating
from the time of James I.*

How Far Is It to Bethlehem?

How far is it to Bethlehem?
  Not very far.
Shall we find the stable-room
  Lit by a star?

Can we see the little child,
  Is he within?
If we lift the wooden latch
  May we go in?

May we stroke the creatures th
  Ox, ass, or sheep?
May we peep like them and see
  Jesus asleep?

If we touch his tiny hand
  Will he awake?
Will he know we've come so
  Just for his sake?

Great kings have precious gif
  And we have naught,
Little smiles and little tears
  Are all we brought.

For all weary children
  Mary must weep.
Here, on his bed of straw
  Sleep, children, sleep.

God in his mother's arms,
  Babes in the byre,
Sleep, as they sleep who find
  Their heart's desire.

HOW FAR IS IT TO BETHLEHEM?

Words by Frances Chesterton
1870–1938

Traditional English tune
Arranged by R. Vaughan Williams

*This very simple folk-tune 'Stowey' is a traditional English melody.
It appears in the children's section of* Songs of Praise *(with different words),
and has become well loved by both children and adults.*

From the *Oxford Book of Carols* by permission of Oxford University Press.
Words by permission of Miss D. E. Collins

IN DULCI JUBILO

Fourteenth-century German carol tune

Harmonised by
R. L. de Pearsall 1795–1856

The melody is found in a German book published in 1570 and is described even then as 'a very ancient song for Christmas Eve'. Both words and tune appear in several early English sources. The words were also printed in Luther's last hymn-book, where the third verse is ascribed to him.

In Dulci Jubilo

1. In dulci jubilo
   Let us our homage shew;
     Our heart's joy reclineth
   In praesepio,
     And like a bright star shineth,
   Matris in gremio.
   Alpha es et O!
   Alpha es et O!

2. O Jesu, parvule,
   I yearn for thee alway!
     Hear me, I beseech thee,
   O puer optime,
     My prayer let it reach thee,
   O princeps gloriae.
   Trahe me post te!
   Trahe me post te!

3. O Patris caritas!
   O Nati lenitas!
     Deeply were we stainèd
   Per nostra crimina;
     But thou has for us gainèd
   Coelorum gaudia.
   O that we were there!
   O that we were there!

4. Ubi sunt gaudia, where,
   If that they be not there?
     There are angels singing
   Nova cantica,
     There the bells are ringing
   In Regis curia.
   O that we were there!
   O that we were there!

Infant Holy, Infant Lowly

Infant holy, Infant lowly,
For his bed a cattle stall;
Oxen lowing, little knowing
Christ the Babe is Lord of all.
Swift are winging, angels singing,
Nowells ringing, tidings bringing,
Christ the Babe is Lord of all,
Christ the Babe is Lord of all.

Flocks were sleeping, shepherds
    keeping
Vigil till the morning new;
Saw the glory, heard the story,
Tidings of a gospel true.
Thus rejoicing, free from sorrow,
Praises voicing, greet the morrow.
Christ the Babe was born for you,
Christ the Babe was born for you.

INFANT HOLY, INFANT LOWLY

Words translated
by Edith M. Reed.

Traditional Polish tune
Arranged by B. V. Burdett

Both the words and tune are traditional Polish. The words of this gentle and touching little carol, with its characteristic rhythm, have been translated from the Polish by Edith M. Reed. (This translation is printed by permission of Evans Brothers Ltd, from the Kingsway Carol Book.*)*

One of Exeter Cathedral's rich collection of corbels.

IN THE BLEAK MID-WINTER

Words by Christina Rossetti
1830–1894

Music by Gustav Holst
1874–1934

Gustav Holst wrote this tune for the newly published English
Hymnal *(1906). The words and music are most beautifully matched and
together have become one of the few really well-known modern carols.
Other modern settings of the words are also becoming popular now.*

Note
*Verses 2, 3, 4 and 5 each contain one or more lines starting with a weak syllable.
Where they occur, these should be sung to the small notes printed with the music.
The slurs indicate where one syllable is sung to two notes.*

By permission of Oxford University Press

Winter in the Mournes, Co. Down

In the Bleak Mid-winter

1. In the bleak mid-winter
     Frosty wind made moan,
   Earth stood hard as iron,
     Water like a stone;
   Snow had fallen, snow on snow,
     Snow on snow,
   In the bleak mid-winter,
     Long ago.

2. Our God, heaven cannot hold him
     Nor earth sustain;
   Heaven and earth shall flee away
     When he comes to reign:
   In the bleak mid-winter
     A stable-place sufficed
   The Lord God Almighty,
     Jesus Christ.

3. Enough for him, whom cherubim
     Worship night and day,
   A breastful of milk,
     And a mangerful of hay;
   Enough for him, whom angels
     Fall down before,
   The ox and ass and camel
     Which adore.

4. Angels and archangels
     May have gathered there,
   Cherubim and seraphim
     Thronged the air:
   But only his mother
     In her maiden bliss
   Worshipped the Belovèd
     With a kiss

5. What can I give him,
     Poor as I am?
   If I were a shepherd
     I would bring a lamb;
   If I were a wise man
     I would do my part;
   Yet what I can I give him –
     Give my heart.

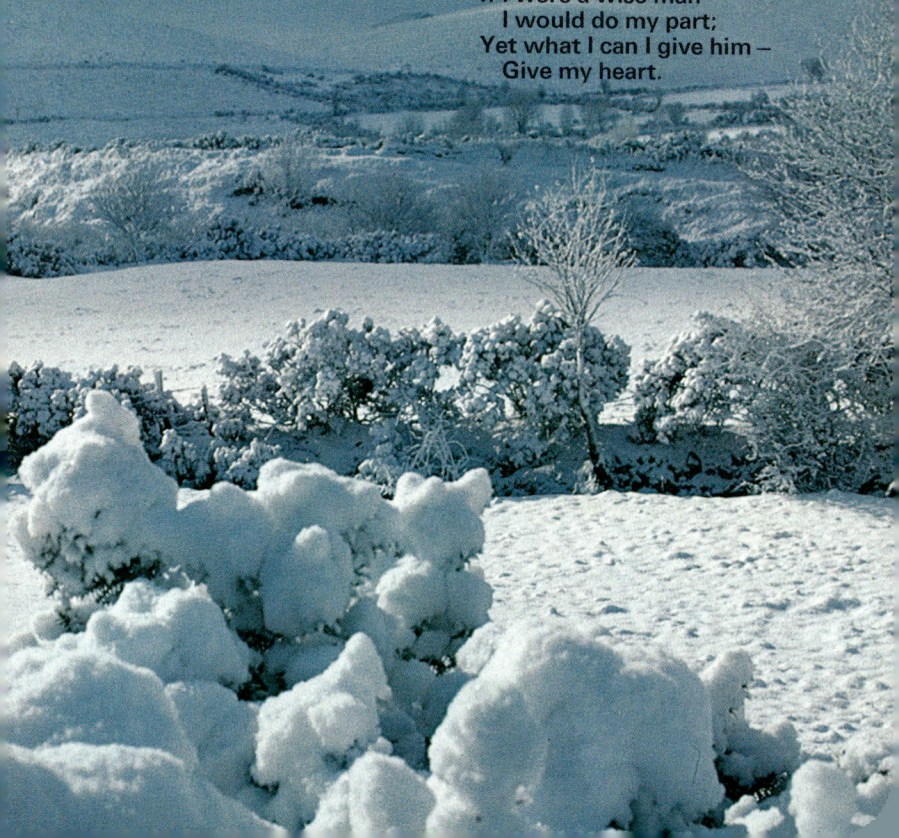

I SAW THREE SHIPS

Words Traditional

Traditional English tune
Arranged by B. V. Burdett

*In one version or another this traditional carol appears in many of the
broadsheets. This version appears in Sandy's Christmas Carols (1833).
A French legend tells how St Mary, sister of the Virgin, and Mary,
mother of James and John together with St Mary Magdalene, fled from
persecution in the Holy Land to France. It is possible that the three
ships may refer to this legend of Les Saintes-Maries-de-la-Mer.*

Clovelly, Devon

I Saw Three Ships

I saw three ships come sailing in,
   On Christmas Day, on Christmas Day,
I saw three ships come sailing in,
   On Christmas Day in the morning.

And what was in those ships all three?
   On Christmas Day, etc.

Our Saviour Christ and his lady.
   On Christmas Day, etc.

Pray, whither sailed those ships all three?
   On Christmas Day, etc.

O, they sailed into Bethlehem.
   On Christmas Day, etc.

And all the bells on earth shall ring,
   On Christmas Day, etc.

And all the angels in Heaven shall sing,
   On Christmas Day, etc.

And all the souls on earth shall sing.
   On Christmas Day, etc.

Then let us all rejoice amain!
   On Christmas Day, etc.

IT CAME UPON
THE MIDNIGHT CLEAR

Words by E. Hamilton Sears
1810–1876

Traditional tune
Harmonised by
Sir Arthur Sullivan 1842–1900

*This splendid tune (Noel) was adapted by Sir Arthur Sullivan from
a tune originally noted down in Herefordshire in 1905. The words
were written by an American Victorian minister, the Reverend Edmund
Hamilton Sears (1810–1876).*

Trafalgar Square

It Came Upon the Midnight Clear

It came upon the midnight clear,
  That glorious song of old,
From angels bending near the earth
  To touch their harps of gold:
'Peace on the earth, goodwill to men,
  From heav'n's all gracious King!'
The world in solemn stillness lay
  To hear the angels sing.

Still through the cloven skies they come,
  With peaceful wings unfurled;
And still their heav'nly music floats
  O'er all the weary world;
Above its sad and lowly plains
  They bend on hov'ring wing;
And ever o'er its Babel sounds
  The blessèd angels sing.

Yet with the woes of sin and strife
  The world has suffered long;
Beneath the angel-strain have rolled
  Two thousand years of wrong;
And man, at war with man, hears not
  The love-song which they bring:
O hush the noise, ye men of strife,
  And hear the angels sing!

For lo! the days are hastening on,
  By prophet-bards foretold,
When, with the ever-circling years,
  Comes round the age of gold;
When peace shall over all the earth
  Its ancient splendours fling,
And the whole world send back the song
  Which now the angels sing.

NOW THE HOLLY BEARS A BERRY

Words from the Cornish
Collated by Percy Deamer

Traditional Cornish tune
Arranged by B. V. Burdett

*Also known as 'Sans Day' or 'St Day' because it was first taken down at St
Day, in the parish of Gwennap, Cornwall. The carol exists both in the Cornish
'Ma gron war'n gelinen' as well as in English.*

From the *Oxford Book of Carols* by permission of Oxford University Press.

34

Now the Holly Bears a Berry

Now the holly bears a berry as white as the milk,
And Mary bore Jesus, who was wrapped up in silk:

Chorus:
And Mary bore Jesus Christ our Saviour for to be,
And the first tree in the greenwood, it was the
   holly, holly! holly!
And the first tree in the greenwood, it was the holly.

Now the holly bears a berry as green as the grass,
And Mary bore Jesus, who died on the cross:

Chorus:

Now the holly bears a berry as black as the coal,
And Mary bore Jesus, who died for us all:

Chorus:

Now the holly bears a berry, as blood is it red,
Then trust we our Saviour, who rose from the dead:

Chorus:

O Come, All Ye Faithful

1.
O come, all ye faithful,
Joyful and triumphant,
O come ye, O come ye to Bethlehem;
Come and behold him,
Born the King of angels:

Chorus:
O come let us adore him,
O come let us adore him,
O come let us adore him,
Christ the Lord.

2.
God of God,
Light of Light,
Lo, he abhors not the Virgin's womb;
Very God,
Begotten not created:

Chorus:

3.
Sing, choirs of angels,
Sing in exultation,
Sing, all ye citizens of heaven above;
Glory to God
In the highest:

Chorus:

4.
Yea, Lord, we greet thee,
Born this happy morning,
Jesu, to thee be glory given;
Word of the Father,
Now in flesh appearing:

Chorus:

O COME, ALL YE FAITHFUL

Words ascribed to J. F. Wade
1711–1786

Composer unknown
probably eighteenth century

This tune was first printed in Samuel Webbe's Essay on the
Church Plainchant *(1782). The words first appeared in* Evening Offices
of the Church *in an edition of 1760, and are thought to have been
written by one John Francis Wade (1711–1786).*

Cambridge

O LITTLE TOWN OF BETHLEHEM

Words by Bishop Phillips Brooks
1835–1893

Music Traditional English
Arranged by R. Vaughan Williams

*This hymn is so well loved that it is now regarded as a carol.
The English traditional tune once called 'The Ploughboy's Dream' was
renamed by Vaughan Williams 'Forest Green', and chosen by him for the
words of Phillips Brooks (1835–1893), Bishop of Massachusetts, a well-known
preacher in America.*

From the *English Hymnal*, by permission of Oxford University Press

Askrigg, Wensleydale

O Little Town of Bethlehem

1. O little town of Bethlehem,
   How still we see thee lie!
   Above thy deep
   And dreamless sleep
   The silent stars go by.
   Yet in thy dark streets shineth
   The everlasting Light;
   The hopes and fears
   Of all the years
   Are met in thee tonight.

2. O morning stars, together
   Proclaim the holy birth,
   And praises sing
   To God the King,
   And peace to men on earth;
   For Christ is born of Mary;
   And, gathered all above,
   While mortals sleep,
   The angels keep
   Their watch of wondering love.

3. How silently, how silently,
   The wondrous gift is given!
   So God imparts
   To human hearts
   The blessings of his heaven.
   No ear may hear his coming;
   But in this world of sin,
   Where meek souls will
   Receive him, still
   The dear Christ enters in.

4. O Holy Child of Bethlehem,
   Descend to us, we pray;
   Cast out our sin,
   And enter in,
   Be born in us today.
   We hear the Christmas angels
   The great glad tidings tell:
   O come to us,
   Abide with us,
   Our Lord Emmanuel.

ONCE IN ROYAL DAVID'S CITY

Words by Mrs Cecil Francis Alexander
1823–1895

Music by H. J. Gauntlett 1805–1876
Harmonised by A. H. Mann 1850–1929

*This carol is often included with children's Christmas hymns but
it is nevertheless also well loved by adults. Mrs C. F. Alexander
(1823–1895) was the wife of Archbishop Alexander, Primate of All Ireland.
John Gauntlett's setting is a first-class example of the best of
Victorian hymn-writing.*

By kind permission of Novello & Co. Ltd

Malvern Abbey,
Hereford and
Worcester

Once in Royal David's City

1.
Once in royal David's city
  Stood a lowly cattle-shed,
Where a mother laid her baby
  In a manger for his bed:
Mary was that mother mild,
Jesus Christ her little child.

2.
He came down to earth from
    heaven
  Who is God and Lord of all,
And his shelter was a stable,
  And his cradle was a stall:
With the poor and mean and lowly
Lived on earth our Saviour holy.

3.
And through all his wondrous
    childhood
  He would honour and obey,
Love and watch the lowly maiden,
  In whose gentle arms he lay:
Christian children all must be
Mild, obedient, good as he.

4.
For he is our childhood's pattern,
  Day by day like us he grew,
He was little, weak, and helpless,
  Tears and smiles like us he knew:
And he feeleth for our sadness.
And he shareth in our gladness.

5.
And our eyes at last shall see him,
  Through his own redeeming love,
For that child so dear and gentle
  Is our Lord in heaven above:
And he leads his children on
To the place where he is gone.

6.
Not in that poor lowly stable,
  With the oxen standing by,
We shall see him; but in heaven,
  Set at God's right hand on high:
Where like stars his children
    crowned
All in white shall wait around.

ON CHRISTMAS NIGHT

Words Traditional

Traditional English tune
Arranged by B. V. Burdett

Both the words and the tune were collected by R. Vaughan Williams from Mrs Verrall at Monks Gate, Sussex. Other versions are found, but this has all the charming freshness and simplicity of a folk song.

Melody and words reprinted by permission of Ursula Vaughan Williams and Oxford University Press.

King's College, Cambridge

On Christmas Night

*The first 2 lines of each verse
should be repeated once.*

On Christmas night all Christians sing,
To hear the news the angels bring,
News of great joy, news of great mirth,
News of our merciful King's birth.

Then why should men on earth be so sad,
Since our Redeemer made us glad,
When from our sin he set us free,
All for to gain our liberty.

When sin departs before his grace,
Then life and health come in its place;
Angels and men with joy may sing,
All for to see the new-born King.

All out of darkness we have light,
Which made the angels sing this night;
'Glory to God and peace to men,
Now and for evermore. Amen'.

PAST THREE A CLOCK

Words by G. R. Woodward
1859–1934

Traditional tune
Harmonised by Charles Wood

The tune is called 'London Waits' and is from W. Chappell's
Popular Music of the Olden Time. *The refrain 'Past three a clock'*
is old, the verses however were written by the Reverend G. R. Woodward
(1859–1934).

By permission of the S.P.C.K.

Big Ben, London

Past Three a Clock

Chorus:
Past three a clock,
And a cold frosty morning:
Past three a clock;
Good morrow masters all!

Born is a Baby, gentle as may be,
Son of th'eternal Father supernal.
Chorus:

Seraph quire singeth, angel bell ringeth;
Hark how they rime it, time it, and chime it.
Chorus:

Mid earth rejoices hearing such voices
Ne'ertofore so well carolling Nowell.
Chorus:

Hinds o'er the pearly dewy lawn early
Seek the high stranger laid in the manger.
Chorus:

Light out of star-land leadeth from far land.
Princes, to meet him, worship and greet him.
Chorus:

Myrrh from full coffer, incense they offer;
Nor is the golden nugget withholden.
Chorus:

Thus they: I pray you, up, sirs, nor stay you
'Till ye confess him likewise, and bless him.
Chorus:

See Amid the Winter's Snow

1. See amid the winter's snow,
   Born for us on earth below;
   See the tender Lamb appears,
   Promised from eternal years:

   Chorus:
   Hail, thou ever-blessed morn;
   Hail, redemption's happy dawn;
   Sing through all Jerusalem,
   Christ is born in Bethlehem.

2. Lo, within a manger lies
   He who built the starry skies;
   He who throned in height sublime
   Sits amid the Cherubim:

   Chorus:

3. Say, ye holy shepherds, say
   What your joyful news today;
   Wherefore have ye left your sheep
   On the lonely mountain steep?

Chorus:

4. 'As we watched at dead of night,
   Lo, we saw a wondrous light;
   Angels singing ''Peace on earth'',
   Told us of the Saviour's birth':

Chorus:

5. Sacred Infant, all divine,
   What a tender love was thine,
   Thus to come from highest bliss
   Down to such a world as this:

Chorus:

6. Teach, O teach us, Holy Child,
   By thy face so meek and mild,
   Teach us to resemble thee,
   In thy sweet humility:

Chorus:

SEE AMID THE WINTER'S SNOW

Words by E. Caswall
1814–1878

Tune by Sir John Goss
1800–1880

*This is another much-loved Christmas hymn of the Victorian period.
Sir John Goss, who wrote this tune, by far the best-known melody
associated with Caswall's words, was a pupil of Thomas-Attwood and
succeeded him as Organist of St Paul's Cathedral.*

*Crina Bottom and
Ingleborough Fell,
North Yorkshire*

SILENT NIGHT

Words by Joseph Mohr
1792–1848

Tune by Franz Gruber
Arranged by B. V. Burdett

The words of this touching little carol were written by Father Joseph Mohr, the Parish Priest of Hallein in the Austrian Tryol, in 1818. The melody was written by Franz Gruber, the local schoolmaster and organist. It was composed for the local church and people because the organ was temporarily out of action. A delightful story in its own right.

Wallgau

Silent Night

Silent night, holy night,
All is calm, all is bright;
Round yon virgin mother and child,
Holy Infant so tender and mild,
Sleep in heavenly peace,
Sleep in heavenly peace.

Silent night, holy night,
Shepherds quake at the sight;
Glories stream from heaven afar
Heavenly hosts sing Alleluia:
Christ the Saviour is born.
Christ the Saviour is born.

Silent night, holy night,
Son of God, love's pure light;
Radiance beams from thy holy face,
With the dawn of redeeming grace;
Jesus, Lord, at thy birth.
Jesus, Lord, at thy birth.

The First Nowell

The first Nowell the angel did say,
Was to certain poor shepherds in fields
  as they lay;
In fields where they lay keeping their
  sheep,
On a cold winter's night that was so
  deep.

Chorus:
Nowell, Nowell, Nowell, Nowell,
Born is the King of Israel.

They lookèd up and saw a star,
Shining in the east, beyond them far,
And to the earth it gave great light,
And so it continued both day and night.

Chorus:

And by the light of that same star,
Three Wise Men came from country far;
To seek for a King was their intent,
And to follow the star wherever it went.

Chorus:

This star drew nigh to the north-west,
O'er Bethlehem it took its rest,
And there it did both stop and stay,
Right over the place where Jesus lay.

Chorus:

Then entered in those Wise Men three,
Full reverently upon their knee,
And offered there, in his presence,
Their gold, and myrrh, and frankincense.

Chorus:

Then let us all with one accord,
Sing praises to our heavenly Lord,
That hath made heaven and earth of
  nought,
And with his blood mankind hath
  bought.

Chorus:

THE FIRST NOWELL

Words Traditional

Traditional tune
Harmonised by Sir John Stainer 1840–1901

*An English traditional carol dating from the seventeenth
century, probably more suitable for Epiphany time. The words and
tune are taken from Sandys's Christmas Carols (1833), with certain
verses left out in common with later versions which appeared.*

Kentmere Valley, Cumbria

THE HOLLY AND THE IVY

Words Traditional

Traditional English tune
Arranged by B. V. Burdett

A very well-loved English folk-carol. The words and tune were collected by Cecil Sharp in Chipping Campden, Gloucestershire, with some additional words from East Harptree in Somerset. Early printed versions date from c. 1710. The subject symbolising the (male) Holly and (female) Ivy is no doubt of ancient pagan origin.

By kind permission of Novello & Co. Ltd

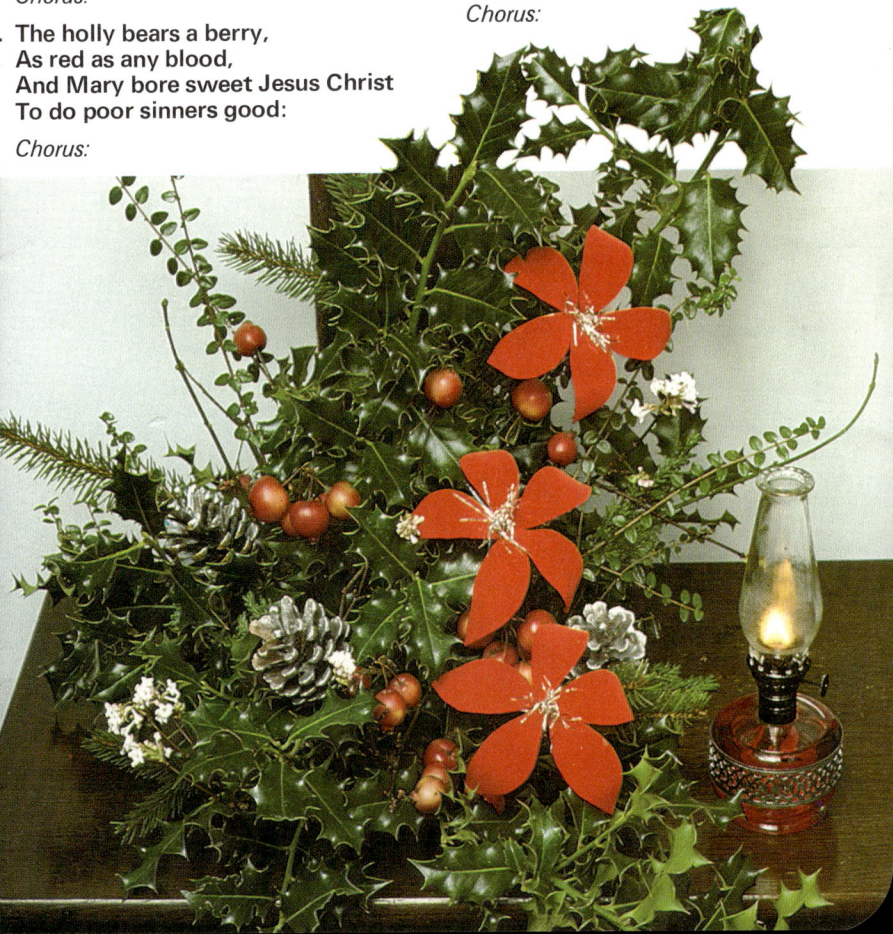

The Holly and the Ivy

The holly and the ivy,
When they are both full grown,
Of all the trees that are in the wood,
The holly bears the crown:

Chorus:
The rising of the sun
And the running of the deer,
The playing of the merry organ,
Sweet singing in the choir.

The holly bears a blossom,
As white as the lily flower,
And Mary bore sweet Jesus Christ
To be our sweet Saviour:

Chorus:

The holly bears a berry,
As red as any blood,
And Mary bore sweet Jesus Christ
To do poor sinners good:

Chorus:

4. The holly bears a prickle,
As sharp as any thorn,
And Mary bore sweet Jesus Christ
On Christmas day in the morn:

Chorus:

5. The holly bears a bark,
As bitter as any gall,
And Mary bore sweet Jesus Christ
For to redeem us all:

Chorus:

6. The holly and the ivy,
When they are both full grown,
Of all the trees that are in the wood,
The holly bears the crown:

Chorus:

THE TWELVE DAYS OF CHRISTMAS

Traditional English

Based on version of Frederic Austin
Rearranged by B. V. Burdett

This very old counting song dates from a thirteenth-century manuscript called 'Twelfth Day', and the words also appear in a children's book, Mirth without Mischief, *dated about 1780. The version used here is that most popularly known, and as remembered by Frederick Austin from his childhood and published in 1909.*

By kind permission of Novello & Co. Ltd

Verse 5

On the fifth day of Christmas my true love sent to me

Five gold rings · Four colly birds, Three French hens

two turtle doves, and a partridge in a pear tree

Verses 6-12

On the twelfth / eleventh / tenth / ninth / eighth / seventh / sixth day of Christmas my

true love sent to me six geese a-laying

Twelve drummers drumming
Eleven pipers piping
Ten lords a-leaping
Nine ladies dancing
Eight maids a-milking
Seven swans a-swimming
Six geese a-laying

continue at †

[Repeat this bar as necessary]

The Twelve Days of Christmas

On the first day of Christmas my true love sent to me –
A partridge in a pear tree.

On the second day of Christmas my true love sent to me –
Two turtle doves and a partridge in a pear tree.

On the third day of Christmas my true love sent to me –
Three French hens, two turtle doves and a partridge in a pear tree.

On the fourth day of Christmas my true love sent to me –
Four colly birds, three French hens, etc.

On the fifth day of Christmas my true love sent to me –
Five gold rings, four colly birds, etc.

On the sixth day of Christmas my true love sent to me –
Six geese a-laying, five gold rings, etc.

On the seventh day of Christmas my true love sent to me –
Seven swans a-swimming, six geese a-laying, etc.

On the eighth day of Christmas my true love sent to me –
Eight maids a-milking, seven swans a-swimming, etc.

On the ninth day of Christmas my true love sent to me –
Nine ladies dancing, eight maids a-milking, etc.

On the tenth day of Christmas my true love sent to me –
Ten lords a-leaping, nine ladies dancing, etc.

On the eleventh day of Christmas my true love sent to me –
Eleven pipers piping, ten lords a-leaping, etc.

On the twelfth day of Christmas my true love sent to me –
Twelve drummers drumming, eleven pipers piping, etc.

St. Peter Mancroft, Norwich

UNTO US IS BORN A SON

Words translated by
G. R. Woodward 1848–1934

Tune from *Piae Cantiones* 1582
Arranged by B. V. Burdett

*This carol is probably of fourteenth-century German origin, certainly
many fifteenth-century German sources exist. The tune in its form here is
in* Piae Cantiones *(1582). Many translations have been made of the words.
The Reverend G. R. Woodward's version is probably the best known and is
used here.*

From the *Cowley Carol Book* by G. R. Woodward and C. Wood, by permission of
A. R. Mowbray & Co. Ltd

"Adoration
the Magi"
Rubens; King
Colle
Chap
Cambrid

Unto Us Is Born a Son

Unto us is born a Son,
  King of quires supernal;
See on earth his life begun,
  Of lords the Lord eternal,
  Of lords the Lord eternal.

Christ, from heav'n descending low,
  Comes on earth a stranger:
Ox and ass their owner know
  Becradled in the manager.

This did Herod sore affray,
  And grievously bewilder;
So he gave the word to slay,
  And slew the little childer.

Of his love and mercy mild
  This the Christmas story:
And O that Mary's gentle Child
  Might lead us up to glory.

O and A and A and O,
  Cum cantibus in choro,
Let our merry organ go,
  Benedicamus Domino.

WE THREE KINGS

Words and tune by J. H. Hopkins
1820–1891

Arranged by Martin Shaw

*This carol was both written and composed about 1857 by Dr J. H. Hopkins
(1820–1891), Rector of Christ's Church, Williamsport, Pennsylvania. This
is another example of a successful modern carol. Each of the kings in
turn presents his gift to the Christ-child.*

From the *Oxford Book of Carols* by permission of Oxford University Press

Westminster Abbey

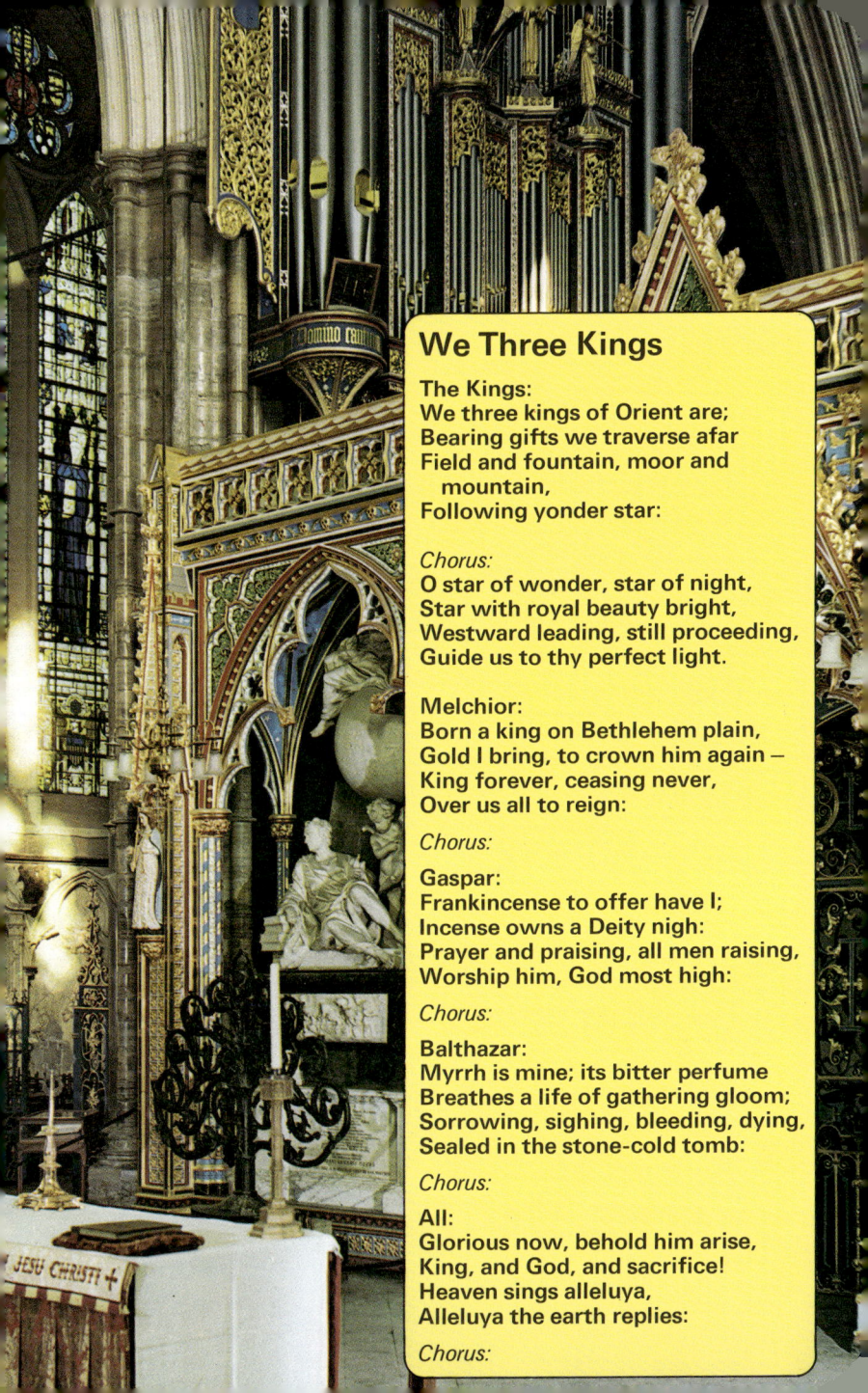

We Three Kings

The Kings:
We three kings of Orient are;
Bearing gifts we traverse afar
Field and fountain, moor and
   mountain,
Following yonder star:

Chorus:
O star of wonder, star of night,
Star with royal beauty bright,
Westward leading, still proceeding,
Guide us to thy perfect light.

Melchior:
Born a king on Bethlehem plain,
Gold I bring, to crown him again –
King forever, ceasing never,
Over us all to reign:

Chorus:

Gaspar:
Frankincense to offer have I;
Incense owns a Deity nigh:
Prayer and praising, all men raising,
Worship him, God most high:

Chorus:

Balthazar:
Myrrh is mine; its bitter perfume
Breathes a life of gathering gloom;
Sorrowing, sighing, bleeding, dying,
Sealed in the stone-cold tomb:

Chorus:

All:
Glorious now, behold him arise,
King, and God, and sacrifice!
Heaven sings alleluya,
Alleluya the earth replies:

Chorus:

WHILE SHEPHERDS WATCHED

Words by Nahum Tate
1652–1715

Tune from *Este's Psalter*
1592

Nahum Tate (1652–1715) wrote the words of this carol, based on St Luke 2: 8–14, which first appeared in 1700 in the earliest supplement to the version of the Metrical Psalms he produced with Nicholas Brady. These words are now associated with the tune 'Winchester Old' from Este's Psalter of 1592 rather than with the traditional tune, not unlike 'God rest you merry' with which they first appeared.

While Shepherds Watched

1.
While shepherds watched their
   flocks by night,
  All seated on the ground,
The angel of the Lord came down,
  And glory shone around.

2.
'Fear not,' said he for mighty dread
  Had seized their troubled mind;
'Glad tidings of great joy I bring
  To you and all mankind.

3.
'To you in David's town this day
  Is born of David's line
A Saviour, who is Christ the Lord;
  And this shall be the sign.

4.
'The heavenly Babe you there shall
   find
  To human view displayed,
All meanly wrapped in swathing
   bands,
  And in a manger laid.'

5.
Thus spake the seraph; and
   forthwith
  Appeared a shining throng
Of angels praising God, who thus
  Addressed their joyful song:

6.
'All glory be to God on high,
  And to the earth be peace;
Good will henceforth from heaven
   to men
  Begin and never cease.'

The Publishers would like to thank the many people whose help and advice have contributed to the make up of this book and particularly those who have allowed their illustrations, words and music to be included.

ISBN 0–7117–0326–4
© 1987 Jarrold Colour Publications
Published and printed in Great Britain by Jarrold & Sons Ltd, Norwich   487